Going Up Higher Declarations for Kids

By: Dr. Amanda Goodson

and Jelonni Goodson

TM

Spiritual *Quick* Books

ISBN-13:978-0615626086

ISBN-10:0615626084

Printed in the U.S.A.

First Edition

Going Up Higher Declarations for Kids

By: Dr. Amanda Goodson

and Jelonni Goodson

TM

Spiritual
Quick Books

TABLE OF CONTENTS

Acknowledgments

A note from Jelonni Goodson to his family, friends and school:

I would like to first give thanks to God for His grace.

To all the parents out there, especially mine, thank you for making sacrifices for us so we can get a good education. To my grandmothers, aunts, uncles, other family and friends – thank you!

I would also like to give thanks Mr. Dowdle, the staff, and teachers of CCS for inspiring me to write. Also, I would like to thank my Sunday school teacher Mrs. Diane Snell for encouraging me.

I would also like to thank a hero in my life Dr. Martin Luther King Jr. because he fought for civil rights and equality among all people.

To my classmates and friends it has been great to know you all. Our experience at CCS is like cheese on a cheeseburger - we stuck together as a family.

Thanks again to all my teachers past and present (especially Mrs. Ford) for inspiring me to write this book with my mom!

Jelonni Goodson

Thanks to my loving husband who loves me unconditionally and supports me continually. To my son, who I affectionately love – thank you for your energy. To my mother and sister, I love you!

To the ministry team who diligently prays declarations daily – thank you for the hours of prayer – may God continue to richly bless you.

Thanks to the readers of these declarations. I pray that the Holy Spirit will pour out His power and love upon you during your time of meditation and reflection with God.

Dr. Amanda Goodson

FORWARD

Declarations for Going Up Higher for Kids will be a useful tool in the hands of kids who are eager to live in God's presence and have a desire to do what is pleasing in His sight. It will give them the opportunity to freely open up to the treasures of God's love and experience a remarkable relationship with the Father by being able to draw close to Him.

Through this experience, each child will be able to come into the presence of God with openness and honesty. They will be able to express themselves to Him and fearlessly declare and assert who they are before Him.

This type of book will richly bless each child as their faith is cultivated and deepened through the daily exercises of spending time in prayer and making declarations. The expectation is that, as their faith is increased through a sincere and direct fellowship with God, they will grow in His love, believe and never doubt that they have free access to all of His promises, and be able to stand to represent Him before the nations as true believers and ambassadors of the King.

"...And a little child shall lead them." (Isaiah 11:6b)

Rosalyn D. Chapple

INTRODUCTION

Dr. Amanda Goodson and her son Jelonni have written *Declarations for Going Up Higher for Kids*, which is designed specifically for kids to be able to declare daily victory in their lives. The book presents a path for spiritual growth and development for children with an inclusion of spiritual prayers and declarations. There is also a challenge for each child to begin meditating and studying the Word of God. These declarations are to be read out loud daily.

With the ever increasing rise in crime and violence in many of our communities and schools, and with so many of our children's lives being at risk, it is essential for them to be able to establish a positive, peaceful, and God-centered position. The aim of this book is to create an environment where God gives each child that opportunity. At the end of each section is a prayer for the child to recite.

Our children of today are tomorrow's kings and queens, and through this vehicle they are challenged daily to speak forth, out loud, their destiny in total agreement with God's Word.

<u>Daily Prayer</u>

Lord, I believe in Jesus in my heart and confess Him with my mouth. He is my Savior and my Lord. I look to Jesus to help me live my life. Please forgive me when I do wrong. I try to live right and love everybody. I obey my parents, pray every day and read my bible. I thank God for keeping me safe every day. I choose friends that love Jesus like I do. In the morning when I wake up, I pray to Jesus for my day to be good. At night before I sleep, I pray to Jesus for my night to be peaceful. During the day, I pray for God to be with me and help me in every way. Keep me from evil and evil from me. Let Your will be done in me and around me. Send Your angels to protect me in all my ways. In Jesus' Name, I pray. Amen.

1. When I wake up in the morning, and before I go to bed at night

- Good morning God. I thank Jesus for waking me up today.

- Thank You God for making this day for me to be happy, no matter what else happens.

- I pray to God daily.

- I follow Jesus. I spend time in saying "thank you" every day.

- Jesus will tell me what to do today in His will.

- I am happy and strong. Jesus makes me stronger day by day.

- I sleep at night and will not have bad dreams.

- I do not have bad thoughts when I go to sleep and when I wake up in the morning.

- Every day is a good day, God made this day for me to enjoy.

- I have peace in my home at night and in the morning.

- I will say this is a new day and that I am happy.

- I enjoy the day that God has created for me.

- I pray for my family every morning and night.

- I am happy God created me.

- I am happy God made heaven and earth.

Prayer:

Lord, thank You for being with me all day long. You are my source of life morning, noon and night. I love You today. Amen.

2. *Anytime during the day*

- I believe Jesus died for my sins.

- I make Jesus first place in my heart.

- I listen to my parents and read the bible to know how I should think.

- My family is a good family.

- God keeps us safe every day and every night.

- God is with us everywhere we go.

- I like to smile and laugh. I know I am a winner. Winners obey parents, do their work and help others.

- I obey my parents and other people that God sends to help me to live better for Jesus.

- God has made me special. There is no one else with the special abilities like me.

- I use my special abilities to do what the bible says I should do.

- I pray and read my bible every day. I say "Thank You, Lord," and ask God to show me the truth.

- I have friends that believe in Jesus as Lord. God sends me friends that love Him.

- I help in my church. I use my voice to sing, my hands to help, and my time to do what is needed in the church and in my home.

- When I am asked to help, I help with a good attitude.

- I look for God to show me His truth. I try to be good; I do not get mad easily; I believe in God, even when other people are mean to me. I pray every day and ask God to help me with everything.

- I love God, my parents, and people God sends to help me. I say, "I apologize," when I do something wrong.

- I do not act like everybody else. I do not act like the people on TV, in movies and in video games. I do what the bible says I should do.

- If I make a mistake, I try to do better the next time. I ask God to help me be a better person.

- When I mention the Name of Jesus, He hears me.

- When someone tries to bully me or try to get me to do something wrong, I say "NO." I get help from godly adults.

- God loves me. God will ask me to do things to help out.

- I am happy every day.

- I believe Jesus can fix any problem.

- I do everything, believing that He can fix everything that is wrong.

- I am strong in my mind.

- I think good things about myself.

- I think that I am smart, even when I have to work hard at it.

- I do not complain when I have to work hard at something.

- I will not let TV, music, video games or anything else keep me from reading my bible and praying every day.

- I do not get too excited.

- I save some of my money for a later date.

- Jesus died on the cross to save my life.

- My teachers speak well of my actions and my schoolwork.

- God made me good. I am a good person.

- I study the bible.

- I think about what the bible says every day.

- I tell people about Jesus. I tell them that Jesus loves them.

- I study to make good grades in school.

- I trust God in my heart.

- I am a warrior for God, and I do not quit.

- I hang in there through hard times.

- I know I will be a tree that will bear good fruit.

- I listen for God's voice when I make decisions.

- I make Godly choices every day.

- I spread God's Word by telling others about Jesus.

Prayer:

Lord God, forgive me of my sins. I repent of my wrongdoing. Please guide my life every day. I need you in my life. Amen.

3. When I am sad or lonely

- I am special to God. God helps me, even when I am sad.

- I am safe with God.

- God has a path for my life. I ask God to show me His path.

- I live in faith. I will not fear. God does not want me to be afraid.

- God wants me to be strong, loving and have good thoughts in my mind.

- I am not afraid.

- I do not think less of myself.

- I do not doubt Jesus in my life.

- I am not alone, God is always there. He lives in my heart.

Prayer:

Lord, thank You for being my light every day. You protect me with from all hurt. You give me favor with You and others. I look to You to lead my life. Amen.

4. *When I am sick*

- I am in good health. Jesus heals me when I am sick.

- I think good thoughts and my body is healed.

- I do not worry.

- Everything in my body is good.

- I eat foods that are good for my body.

- I have a good, healthy heart.

- I pray to God to heal my body.

- I will go to the doctor when I am sick. I will follow what they say.

- I count on the Lord. He already healed me.

- I am secure because Jesus is in me.

- No weapon that is formed against me can win.

- I do what is in God's will, not mine own will.

- Jesus came that I might have life.

- When I am in pain, I confess the Word of God for the pain to leave my body.

Prayer:

Thank You, Lord for Your healing power. Deliver me and show me Your strength in my body and spirit. Amen.

5. When I am angry

- I am patient.

- I do not get angry.

- I am not a sad person. I am a happy person.

- I believe that Jesus hears me when I pray.

- I believe the Lord will help me to not get angry.

- When I am angry, I do not argue. I take a deep breath and forget about it.

- I forgive others, no matter what.

- I go to God when I am not treated fairly; He will help me handle my problems.

- I tell my parents when things go wrong.

- I do not get frustrated, but I will be content.

- I ask for forgiveness for any one I have hurt or who hurt me.

- I do not let anger take over me.

- I keep myself calm at all times.

- I am slow to get angry.

- I do not say bad words to anyone.

- I am thankful for what God has given me.

- I use kind words when I talk. I am not a rude, angry person.

- I do not get upset for long periods of time.

Prayer:

Thank You, God for making me a peaceful, kind and strong person. I am happy, and I am slow to get angry. I thank You for Jesus and for His love for me. Amen.

6. What God says about me

- I am loved by God.

- Jesus is my friend.

- Jesus lives in my heart.

- I am wonderfully made.

- I am marvelous in God's eyes.

- I am carefully made by God. God knew me before I was born.

- I am accepted by Him.

- I am adopted as His son/daughter.

- I am forgiven.

- I belong to Jesus Christ.

- I have godly wisdom.

- I understand hard things.

- I have blessings from Him in heaven.

- I can speak to tough problems, and they will go away if I believe in Him.

Prayer:

God, You call me a son/daughter. Thank You for making me a wonderful person with a positive attitude. I am godly in my actions, and I speak what the Word of God says about me, in Jesus' name I pray. Amen.

These declarations are binding by the blood of Jesus, the Word of God, the authority of the Name of Jesus, the power of the Holy Spirit, and the word of my testimony in agreement/alignment with the Word of God. Hallelujah! Amen!!

Declarations for Daily Living (Scripture References)

Instructions: Write down each scripture below and become familiar with them.

1. When I wake up in the morning and before I go to bed at night

- Psalm 118:24

- Psalm 91

- Psalm 37:23

- Nehemiah 8:10

2. Anytime during the day

- 1 Corinthians 2:16

- 1 Corinthians 13

- Matthew 6:33

- Song of Solomon 6:9

- Galatians 5:19-24

- 1 Corinthians 13:11

- Malachi 3:10-12

- Luke 6:38

- 2 Corinthians 9:6-8

- Ephesians 6:10-18

- Matthew 5:8-9; Psalm 24:3-5

- Romans 12:2

- Revelation 2:5

- Luke 10:19

- Ephesians 4:23

- Philippians 4:19

- Matthew 19:26

- Philippians 4:13

- Jeremiah 29:11-13

- John 10:10

- Isaiah 53:5

- 1 John 1:7

- 2 Corinthians 9:10

- Galatians 3:13

- Luke 2:52

- Psalm 139:14-16

- Matthew 28:18-20

- 2 Corinthians 1:21-22

- 1 John 2:20

- 1 John 2:27

3. When I am sad or lonely

- Zechariah 2:8

- Genesis 6:8

- Zephaniah 2:3

- John 15:2-4

- 2 Timothy 1:7

- Matthew 14:31

- James 3:13-18

4. *When I am sick*

- Isaiah 53:5

- Philippians 1:28

- Isaiah 53:5

- Isaiah 53:5

- Isaiah 53:5

- Mark 16:18b

- Psalm 19:1

- Ephesians 1:3-13

5. *When I am angry*

- Philippians 4:6-7

- 2 Corinthians 10:5

- Mark 5:25-26

6. *What God says about me*

- Psalm 139:14

- Jeremiah 1:1-5

- Ephesians 1:3-14

- Mark 11:24-26

Notes

BIBLIOGRAPHY

New American Standard Bible, Updated Edition, 1995.

Exhaustive Concordance of the Bible. (Lahabra, CA: The Lockman Foundation -- Foundation Publications, Inc. Anaheim, CA); 1981, 1998.

The Spirit Filled Bible (NKJV). (Nelson Publishing), 2002.

About the Authors:

Dr. Amanda H. Goodson and Jelonni Goodson

Are both   natives of Decatur, Alabama and currently reside in Tucson, Arizona. Dr. Goodson serves as pastor. She also plans and facilitates seminars, workshops, and retreats for churches. Jelonni serves in the youth ministry at the church.

Dr. Goodson is President and on the board of Directors for Never the Same Ministries (NTS), a God inspired, Tucson based, Kingdom led ministry dedicated to serve as a vessel through which people are provided tools and resources to develop a more spiritually mature and improved relationship with God through Christ. The NTS God-ordered mission is to provide biblically based instruction, tools and coaching for people within the community through planning and deployment of conferences and events across the United States.

As kingdom citizens, both Dr. Goodson and Jelonni are fully submitted to the will of God. Their prayer is to be active in sharing their faith, make their thoughts agreeable to the will of God, and to have the mind of Christ. The Word of God is the final authority in their lives.

For a complete listing of CDs, DVDs, and books by Dr. Amanda Goodson, or to participate in a ministry conference, book a conference, speaking event or training, please email or visit the following web site:

Ntsministries@aol.com

or visit

ntsministries.org

Books by Dr. Amanda Goodson

Kingdom Character
Spiritual Authority
Carmel Voices
The Power to Make an Impact
Step out in Faith
Powerful People Follow Christ
On the Rise

Back cover photo by: Martha Lochert Photography

www.ingramcontent.com/pod-product-compliance
Lightning Source LLC
Chambersburg PA
CBHW020953030426
42339CB00004B/86